Writing Client Roadmap

A PROVEN PLAN FOR LANDING YOUR FIRST FREELANCE WRITING CLIENTS

Rebecca Livermore

Professional Content Creation

Littleton, Colorado

Writing Client Roadmap

Copyright © 2019 by Rebecca Livermore

ISBN-13: 9781707557165

All rights reserved. No part of this publication may be reproduced, stored in a retrieval system, or transmitted by any means – electronic, mechanical, photographic (photocopying), recording, or otherwise – without prior permission in writing from the author.

Learn more information at: ProfessionalContentCreation.com

Table of Contents

Introduction	1
Chapter 1: Pros and Cons of Client Work	5
Chapter 2: Determine the Type of Writing You Want to Do	13
Chapter 3: Why and How to Specialize	27
Chapter 4: Choose a Business Model	31
Chapter 5: Choose a Business Style	41
Chapter 6: Lay the Foundations for Healthy Client Work	43
Chapter 7: Find Your First Clients	47
Chapter 8: Set the Stage for Growing Your Writing Business	55
Chapter 9: Top 5 Mistakes Freelance Writers Make	61
Resources	77

Introduction

Hello, and welcome to Writing Client Roadmap: A Proven Plan for Landing Your First Freelance Writing Clients.

Have you ever. . .

- Wondered if it's possible to make a living writing?
- Wished you could quit your day job and just write?
- Wanted to start a freelance writing business but don't know how to start?

If so, this book is for you!

My name's Rebecca Livermore, and I'm a fulltime writer. I started freelance writing in 1993, but for many years, I treated my writing as a hobby more than a business. This all changed when eight years ago, I started writing for clients. That one shift is what made it possible for me to quit my day job and write full time.

Sounds great, right? But the big question is, how do you get started writing for clients?

I'm glad you asked! In this book, I dive into how to land your first clients as a freelance writer.

I share a simple roadmap which includes the following basic steps:

- Determine if client work is right for you. In this chapter, I dive into the pros and cons of client work, so that you'll go into client work with your eyes wide open.
- Determine the type of writing you want to do. You'll discover some of the primary content types that you can offer to clients.
- How to choose an area of specialty. You'll learn why specialization matters and how it enables you to land more clients and ultimately build a profitable writing business.
- How to choose both a business model and business style that fit with your personality and dream lifestyle.
- How to lay the foundation for healthy relationships with clients.
- And finally, how to land your first writing clients.

This book is perfect for you if you've dreamed about making a living writing, but up to this point have had limited success.

So what are we waiting for? It's time to get this show on the road!

About this Book

This book is book #2 in the Profitable Writer Series. It's a natural follow up to book #1, *Same Page: A Freelance Writer's Guide to Building Healthy Client Relationships* because once you've laid the proper foundation for building healthy client relationships, it's time to get those first clients. I've intentionally kept the books in this series short and tightly focused so that you don't waste time reading a bunch of fluff.

This book, along with the other books in the series, is focused on action, rather than theory.

Chapter 1: Pros and Cons of Client Work

More than eight years ago, I quit my job to do client work full time. I've written hundreds of blog posts for clients, edited and formatted books, and managed content for some big-name bloggers, authors, and social-media superstars.

I made a good living doing it. I'm deeply grateful for all of the opportunities and life lessons I've gained through client work. I have no regrets for taking on writing clients, and yet in spite of that, I no longer write content for clients.

I share that last bit of information with you not to discourage you, but rather to be honest with you about some of the challenges associated with client work.

With that in mind, in this chapter, I'll share with you both the pros and cons of client work so that you'll have your eyes wide open as you explore this career option.

Pros of Writing Content for Clients

It's always nice to start with the good news, right? So, before I get into the negative aspects of writing content for clients, I want to cover good reasons for taking on writing clients.

Guaranteed Income

First, obviously, is money. Unless you end up working for deadbeat clients, when someone hires you to write content for them, you're guaranteed to make money. Writing your own content may be more fun, but when you do so, you have no guarantee that you'll ever make enough, or for that matter, any money.

For example, I'm writing this book, at least partially by faith. I can pretty well guarantee that the book will sell, but I can't predict with any degree of accuracy how many books I'll sell. There are times when I think a book is destined to succeed, and it does marginally well, or even worse, is a total flop. Other times I feel so uncertain about a particular book that I let it sit gathering dust on my computer. When I finally publish it, I'm surprised by consistent sales.

The bottom line is that when publishing your own content, there are no income guarantees.

In contrast, when you write content for clients, you generally know ahead of time how much you'll make before you even start the work.

Retainer Work Provides Guaranteed Income

The money aspect is especially true if you work on a retainer basis. The client work that I've done has been almost exclusively on retainer. When you work on a retainer, you promise to do a specific amount of work each month in exchange for a set amount of money. This type of business model is what enabled me to quit my day job because I knew that I'd have enough writing income to pay my bills.

Be Part of a Team

Writing is often a lonely game since you spend most, if not all, of your day working alone. When you do client work, you often do it as part of a bigger team. For instance, when I've written content for clients, I've often worked alongside not just the client, but virtual assistants, graphic designers, videographers, etc.

In addition to email or communication inside project management tools, there are often video or phone team meetings. I've also experienced in person-team retreats, attended conferences with team members, and so on. As an introvert, I enjoy the solitude of writing, but also enjoy having teammates.

Learn from Your Clients

The next pro of writing content for clients is that you can learn a lot from your clients.

I've had the privilege of working for some fantastic clients. Much of what I know about social media, WordPress, podcasting, business, and a host of other things came about as a result of client work.

For example, when I worked for Marcus Sheridan, he asked me to figure out podcasting. Not only did he pay me for my time while I learned, I also observed how a master communicator handled podcasting. Marcus is also a great example of someone who knows how to balance faith and family while running a successful business.

When I worked for Amy Porterfield, I improved my podcasting skills even more. I also learned how to create, promote, and conduct webinars and online courses. Planning and thinking big are things at which Amy excels. Most of my ability to combine big dreams with solid plans comes from the time I spent working for her.

Michael Hyatt taught me how to optimize blog posts and how to balance hard work with time to rest and recharge.

I learned a lot about how to think like an entrepreneur while I worked on content for Patrick Bet-David. As an immigrant that at one time lived in a refugee camp and grew up on welfare, he's a great example of how to succeed against all the odds.

I wouldn't know what I know or be who I am today if it wasn't for writing content for clients.

Cons of Writing Content for Clients

In spite of the positive aspects of client work, it's essential to understand the disadvantages of client work as well. Let's dive into some of the drawbacks of writing content for clients that I personally experienced.

Loss of Freedom

First is the loss of freedom.

Over the years, I've come to realize that freedom is one of my core drivers. Money doesn't motivate me nearly as much as freedom. I see money as nothing more than a tool to provide me with the freedom to live where and how I want.

Initially, I saw writing content for clients as a path to freedom. There was some truth to that. Client work enabled me to quit my day job. But it also meant showing up for meetings and doing work that wasn't always to my liking. I also had to, at times, deal with unreasonable deadlines.

I'm in a season of life now where freedom matters more than ever.

Since I let go of client work, I now live where I want, when I want. I also work whatever hours make the most sense for me at the time. My only deadlines are the ones I set for myself.

Loss of Voice

The next con of writing content for clients is loss of voice.

Depending on the type of client work you do, you may write in someone else's voice.

The articles or books you slave over will likely bear someone else's name.

You may have to write in a style that is not your own. In fact, you should write in a style that is not your own if you're creating content that bears a name other than your own.

For example, I wrote a ton of content for top entrepreneur, Patrick Bet-David. Most of the content that I published bore his name. That was totally appropriate, because I based the content on his videos, and the expertise shared was definitely his. I wrote using his personality and in his voice.

Keep in mind that there's technically nothing wrong with this. It's not wrong to write something and have someone else get the credit, particularly when you write content based on their expertise. Many writers make a good living doing just that.

Other writers have their own stories, thoughts, and tips they want to share, and find writing content for others to be soul-crushing. Only you can determine whether or not the loss of voice matters to you.

Low Time or Energy to Create Your Own Content

Next, when you write content for others, you may find you have no time or energy to create your own content.

Now it's true that in most cases, even if you write content for others, you can still write your own books, blog posts, and so on. But at least in my experience, spending four or six intense hours a day writing for others fries my brain. At that point, I don't have it in me to write my own content.

During my years as a content writer for others, my blog languished. I'd publish posts three weeks in a row, and then burn out, and quit. I wrote a book here and there, but most of my book ideas gathered dust. What used to be fun, became drudgery.

This frustrated me because, in theory, I was free to write as much of my content as I desired. There was a disconnect between what I told others to do - publish content consistently - and what I did. I felt guilty because unless I pointed to the content I created for others, my actions didn't match my words.

High Stress Levels

The next con of writing content for others is that depending on the types of writing clients you take on, you may experience high-stress levels.

I was privileged to work for very high-caliber clients. As I mentioned earlier, in no small degree, I am who I am today as a result of the amazing people for whom I worked.

Those amazing people were indeed amazing. And guess what? They didn't get that way by putting out average amounts of content or taking evenings and weekends off.

Most of them worked continuously, and because of that, so did I. I started work early in the morning and dropped into bed exhausted late at night.

Even on weekends, I regularly checked my cell phone for urgent messages, and as needed, dropped everything to address the need of the moment. I seldom truly unplugged.

Now you may work for more balanced clients. In chapter six, I provide some tips on how to lay the foundation for healthy client relationships. By doing so, you may be able to reduce or eliminate the stress of client work.

Trading Time for Money

The next con of client work is that with it, you trade time for money.

That was one of my biggest challenges with writing content for clients.

When I worked, I got paid, and when I didn't work, I didn't get paid. It was like having a job, without benefits like health insurance, paid vacations, and holidays.

The bottom line was that all the writing I did built someone else's business while my own business languished.

Yes, I had a thriving business in the sense that I never had to worry about getting clients. Clients came to me, and I determined whether to take them on. My abundance of client work was a dream for many writers, and it's something for which that even now I thank God.

But in a practical sense, it wasn't sustainable. I hit burnout, and since I neglected my own content in favor of hitting it out of the park with my client's content when I decided to drop client work, I almost had to start over with my own writing.

Dropping client work was scary. But I realized that for me, even though focusing on my content is a much slower path to financial freedom, it's the only path that pays me today and will continue to do so for years to come.

Pro Tip: If you do write content for clients, sock away as much of your earnings as you can in savings and retirement accounts. If you do this, you'll continue to benefit financially long after you stop writing for the clients.

By the way, before I close off this chapter on the pros and cons of writing content for clients, I want to say that in spite of the disadvantages, if you really need consistent income, I recommend client work as the best way to make it as a freelance writer.

With that in mind, in the next chapter, we'll get into how to come up with ideas for the type of writing you can do for clients.

Chapter 2: Determine the Type of Writing You Want to Do

There are so many different types of writing you can do for clients that I'll only scratch the surface in this chapter. Having said that, the ideas in this chapter are varied and provide ample fodder for coming up with ideas that are 100% ideal for you.

Business Blogging

As a business blogger, you'll write content to help build someone else's business. For example, if you were to write content for an investment company, you may write blog posts that have to do with investments. These posts may not mention the company by name but can be used to help people discover the company and potentially do business with them. Essentially, this is content marketing for a company other than your own.

As an example, I had a very lucrative writing gig for a company focused on female bloggers. I wrote three posts per week, week in and week out, so it was a steady source of income. The great thing about it was that I could write on most anything I wanted, as long as it fit with the main categories of the blog.

My content helped attract female bloggers who might then subscribe to the magazine, buy other products, or attend conferences. I never mentioned the company itself in my posts, but people that landed on the site through my blog posts often signed up for the email list or engaged with the company in other ways.

If you want to blog for other businesses, but don't know how to get started, the first step is to start a blog on the topic about which you want to write. (In the next chapter, we'll dive into how and why to choose an area of specialty, so be sure to check that out for more information.)

Once you start your blog, write your very best content on the blog. At the end of each post, include an author bio that includes the fact that you write content for "x" type of business, and include a link to your contact or services page. You can also guest post on prominent blogs in the specific industry you want to target. Just make sure that any site you write for allows you to connect to your website in your bio.

Once you have a substantial selection of blog posts on your site, reach out to companies to see if they need help. Look for companies that either don't have a blog or have an abandoned blog. Either way, it's clear they need help writing blog posts! You can use your blog as a sample of your work.

This type of writing requires some focus on building up your blog and establishing yourself as an expert. It's perfect for you if you are passionate about a topic and would enjoy writing about it consistently.

Email Marketing

Some people say that email marketing is dead, but nothing can be further from the truth. Email is still one of the most popular types of written content, and an email list is one of the most profitable assets of most businesses.

But many business owners struggle when it comes to knowing what to email to their list. Even if they know, they may struggle with finding the time to devote to it regularly.

Because of this, email marketing can be a very lucrative type of writing.

Here are some of the types of emails you can write for clients:

- Monthly or weekly newsletters
- Blog posts announcements
- Autoresponder series, which are pre-written emails that go out on a set schedule to people who purchase a product or sign up for an email list
- Sales-focused emails that highlight products, services, exclusive deals, and so on

This type of writing requires the ability to write sales copy (ideally without sounding salesy) and is perfect for writers that don't mind doing behind-the-scenes work.

Magazine Articles

I got my start writing for print magazines. The great thing about writing for print magazines is that they often pay a very lucrative amount of money for each article. The bad news is that there are now fewer print magazines out there, and writing for them can be very competitive.

However, there's a thrill associated with holding a print magazine in your hand and seeing your name and photo.

If you want to write for print magazines, head to your nearest large bookstore and browse the magazine section. Since big bookstores such as Barnes and Noble are disappearing, if you don't have one near you, head to the best library in your area and check out the magazines. You can also discover magazines that accept submissions in books such as Writer's Market. A new edition comes out each year and provides information such as pay, and how to submit articles to numerous magazines.

Once you identify magazines of interest, become a student of each magazine that grabs your attention. Make a note of the types of articles they publish, including the tone. For instance, are they sarcastic, serious, playful, or academic? What type of people read the magazine? Do they have any writer's guidelines? If so, be sure to grab a copy and study it thoroughly. Follow the guidelines to the letter to keep from being immediately eliminated from consideration.

Learn to write great query letters, as they are often a required part of the process. If your query letter results in a "thanks, but no thanks" response, don't give up. Tweak the query letter to fit another magazine you plan to pitch to so that it fits with their tone and requirements.

Even though print magazines aren't as popular as they once were, a trip to the library - or the grocery checkout - shows that many people still love magazines, so this can be a lucrative writing pursuit.

This type of writing requires persistence and the ability to handle rejection without getting too discouraged. It is perfect for anyone that enjoys a lot of variety and loves seeing their name in print, not to mention holding tangible evidence of their writing success in their hands.

Copywriting

Copywriting, in short, is writing sales copy. It can take the form of sales pages on websites, promotional emails, ad copy, lead magnets, and so on. Since it has the potential to make people money, it is one of the most lucrative types of writing you can do for clients.

Before you jump on the copywriting bandwagon, it's essential to understand that it's half art and half science. Even many experienced copywriters spend many hours on a single page of copy, tweaking each word.

Since copywriting is a specialized skill, I recommend investing in training and then practicing copywriting with your own content. For instance, put what you learn into practice on your homepage, lead magnets, sales pages, promotional emails, book descriptions, and so on. Keep track of what works and what doesn't, and tweak things.

Applying copywriting skills to your content accomplishes two primary things. First, it enables you to become an expert copywriter. Second, it helps you sell more of your own products and services. The second reason alone provides you with good enough reason to work on mastering this skill, even if you never offer it as a service. In short, all writers should learn copywriting, and those who learn it well can offer it as a service to others.

Here are a few recommended resources for learning copywriting:

- Ben Settle: http://www.bensettle.com. Opt into his email list to observe firsthand how he handles promotional emails.
- How to Write Copy That Sells: The Step-By-Step System for More Sales, to More Customers, More Often by Ray Edwards
- Copywriting For Beginners: How To Write Web Copy That Sells Without Being Cheesy, which you can get at https://skl.sh/2PBAAM4. (Note that this one is a Skillshare premium course. If you do not currently have a Skillshare premium account, you can use my referral link to get a free, two-month trial: https://www.professionalcontentcreation.com/skillshare.)

Copywriting requires practice and training to perfect but has the potential to be very lucrative. It is perfect for writers that enjoy the marketing aspect of writing.

Newsletters

I've already mentioned newsletters under email marketing. To be sure, most newsletters are now sent out via email, but some companies and nonprofits send out monthly or quarterly newsletters via good old-fashioned snail mail.

As much as we love digital content, you can more easily read some content when in print. This is especially true if the content is detailed in nature, with charts, graphs, and other visuals. Print versions of newsletters are also helpful for businesses and ministries that target older adults who may be less comfortable with digital media. Local businesses can also benefit from print newsletters, especially if they add coupons to the newsletters.

If you want to give this type of writing a try, I recommend signing up for newsletters sent out by your favorite businesses and causes. Study the ones you receive. See how they differ from the digital information the same companies send out.

This type of writing may require more footwork on your part in being proactive in landing clients. It's perfect for you if you want to differentiate yourself from other writers that focus exclusively on digital content.

White Papers

According to this article on Wikipedia, https://en.wikipedia.org/wiki/White_paper, "A white paper is an authoritative report or guide that informs readers concisely about a complex issue and presents the issuing body's philosophy on the matter. It is meant to help readers understand an issue, solve a problem, or make a decision."

White papers are professional in tone, well-researched, and fact-based.

Check out this in-depth blog post by CoSchedule on how to write white papers: https://coschedule.com/blog/how-to-write-white-papers-templates-examples/.

This type of writing requires strong research skills and the ability to synthesize information in a way that is accurate but compelling. Writing white papers is perfect for people who enjoy research and have excellent attention to detail, as well as the ability to share information in a clear, logical manner.

Case Studies

Case studies are similar to white papers in that they are both researched-based. However, case studies tend to have a narrower focus. I love the way that "That White Paper Guy" defines case studies in this article: https://thatwhitepaperguy.com/white-paper-article-white-papers-and-case-studies/. He says, "*A case study is like looking down through a magnifying glass at one flower. You focus in on one company in particular, telling the story of how it benefitted from using a certain product or service. A white paper is like looking up through a telescope at a whole galaxy in space. You tell the story of how an entire industry has been suffering from a certain problem and propose a better way to solve it.*"

What I love about case studies is that you can conduct and present case studies on your own business. You can then point to them as examples of the types of case studies you can write for others.

If you also like to come up with writing (and other forms of content) plans, you can use your case-study-writing skills to report the results to your clients. As an example, when I was hired to write content for a site, the client was very focused on numbers. So, as I did the work, I documented the results of my work. The primary focus of my case study was the results my writing had on his website traffic, including things such as overall traffic, page views, time on site, and so on.

The case study was an effective way to show the value of the work that I did. Also, since I paid attention to the results of the work I did, it helped me to know better what was and wasn't working. I share this to illustrate that in addition to being a type of service you can offer to clients, you can also provide case studies to your clients to help them see the value of your services.

In my opinion, case studies can also be less formal in tone than white papers. (Disclaimer: I've never written white papers, but I have written some case studies. While my case studies are researched-based, they are somewhat conversational in tone, similar to my regular blog posts.)

If you'd like a few examples of case studies, check out this post on the Smart Passive Income blog: https://www.smartpassiveincome.com/3-online-business-case-studies-inspired-by-the-spi-community/

Writing case studies requires the ability to research and analyze information and then present your findings in an enjoyable manner. If you like doing research, analyzing the findings, and presenting your conclusions in a professional but relaxed style, writing case studies may be perfect for you.

Ghostwriting Books and Blog Posts

I have experience ghostwriting both books and blog posts. For instance, I wrote a few books based on my pastor's sermons. I started by transcribing them. Next, I went through and cut out anything that didn't quite fit, such as bunny trails. I then put them into a more solid written form.

I had another client that is a YouTube superstar. He creates amazingly helpful YouTube videos that are chock full of useful content. He's a brilliant man, but he's not a writer. In the same way, as with the books I ghostwrote, I started by transcribing the videos. (This had the added benefit of being able to upload the transcripts as subtitles on the videos.) I then took the transcripts and created headings for the main points. I cut out anything that didn't quite fit or wasn't as helpful and got the content into solid, grammatically correct, written form.

Finally, I offered a service that I called "Blogging Your Voice." I share about this in detail in Chapter 4: Choose a Business Model because you can create an entire business off this one service. The fundamental way it worked is that I interviewed clients and then wrote blog posts based on the interviews.

As you can see from the examples above, you can ghostwrite content in two primary ways. First, you can take content that already exists, such as speeches, videos, courses, and so on, and use it as the basis for your written content. You can also interview people to get the information you need and then write the content from there. A key thing to keep in mind when ghostwriting is to use the client's exact words as much as possible. The goal is to sound "just like" your client, only better.

This type of writing requires the ability to get inside someone's head and write like they talk. When you ghostwrite, the goal is to put aside your own writing style and take on a style that has the personality and "voice" of your client. This type of writing is perfect for you if you enjoy learning new things and helping others shine. It's also essential to be willing to be in the background, as your name may not appear on your work.

Tutorials

Have you ever tried to follow poorly written instructions? Most often, this happens in manuals where the product was produced outside of the United States and yet sold to U.S. consumers. I'm sure you've also had the opposite experience where instructions were clearly written, along with screenshots with annotations. The latter reduces the frustration for users of a product (including software). They also make it possible for the customer to have a much more positive experience with the product. Not only does this increase customer retention odds, it also makes the customers more likely to share the product with friends and family. Because of this, while tutorials may seem dry and dull, they are incredibly helpful, and many companies are more than happy to pay to produce them.

The best way to land your first tutorial-writing clients is to first start with products that you personally use. For instance, if you use a bookkeeping system, check to see if they have written instructions. If they have video tutorials only, go through one of the instructional videos and create written instructions as a sample. Approach the company with your sample and see if they might be interested in hiring you to create written tutorials to go with the rest of the training videos.

While it can take time to create the written tutorial without any promise of landing the gig, I believe the benefits of it outweigh the risks. For one thing, you have a solid sample that gives the company an idea of how much value your services bring to the table. In addition to that, if you track your time while creating the sample, you'll have a clear idea of how much time the project will take and can create a proposal that more accurately takes into account the amount of work the project will require.

You can also make the case that while video tutorials can be beneficial, some people learn better by reading than listening or watching videos. In addition to that, even if people like video content, it can take less time to read step-by-step instructions with screenshots than it does to watch an entire video. Sell potential clients on the customer satisfaction benefits of offering tutorials using more than one medium.

If you desire to focus on this type of writing, you may want to create a website with a blog where you produce a lot of tutorials. You can bill yourself as a tech writer or tutorial queen, and provide information on how people can hire you.

As your portfolio of samples (in the form of blog posts) grows, you can direct potential clients to your website to see your work. That will save time compared to creating sample tutorials specific to the company, as I mentioned above. In addition to that, you can monetize your blog content by using affiliate links for the products for which you create tutorials.

There are a couple of great tools to use for creating great-looking tutorials, with Snagit being my top choice.

This type of writing requires the ability to make complicated things simple and easy to understand. It also requires a small amount of technical expertise in using tools such as Snagit. Writing tutorials is great for people who enjoy reading instruction books, have attention to detail, and enjoy teaching people how to use products.

Content Strategist

Content strategy goes beyond merely writing content for clients. It's sitting down and creating a plan for using content to grow a business. In a sense, you can put it into the writing bucket because it typically involves a written plan. You may also do some of the actual writing since written content can be a large part of the plan. The plan you create for people may include content creation that goes beyond your area of expertise. For instance, you may include social media, course content, YouTube videos and so on in the plan.

In my opinion, content strategy is something that should come later in your career as a freelance writer. This matters because you need to have a solid foundation in understanding how to grow a business with content. You also need to have proven experience in doing so. The good news is, you can gain that experience creating content for your site and then apply what you learn to creating content strategies for clients. For example, you may master blogging, including blog monetization strategies. Even with that level of experience, you can create a blogging strategy for clients, based on the success of your own blog.

It's possible that like me, you've worked on a team with other content creators. For instance, I've worked on a team where I handled written content, and another part of the team handled video production, and yet another part of the team handled social media. Even though I was "just" the writer, since we all worked together, I learned a lot about how to integrate the other types of content into a cohesive content strategy.

By the way, since no one is good at everything, it's best to create a strategy and then work only in your area of strength - writing. If you happen to get hired as a content manager, hire out people who specialize in your weak areas.

This type of writing requires you to have a solid grasp on how to use many aspects of content to grow a business. It's best for people with content marketing skills and experience. This is perfect for people who want to take their services up a notch by providing consulting and potentially team management in addition to actual writing.

Chapter 3: Why and How to Specialize

In this chapter, we'll dive into how to brainstorm your skills, experience, and interests and then use that information to help you land writing clients.

Here's the deal. While you can technically write on almost any topic, it makes sense to target potential writing clients of a specific industry.

In other words, rather than writing content on personal finance, entrepreneurship, dog grooming, and faith, pick one area and become known as THE writer on that and related topics.

Let's get into why specialization makes sense.

Why Specialize

Become Known as an Expert

The first reason I recommend specializing in a specific industry is that you'll become known as an expert in your field of choice. For example, you can become known as a personal finance writer, or a health writer, or a business writer. There's a certain clout to being known for a specific type of writing.

You can't "eat" clout, but you can take the higher earnings associated with being a specialist to the bank.

Get More Referrals

Second, if you specialize in a specific field, you're likely to get more referrals. Let's face it; people in particular industries rub shoulders with others in the same industry. If you, for example, write for a couple of top-notch entrepreneurs, when their peers are looking for a writer, your name will likely come up. I've experienced my name coming up again and again among those who have online businesses because many of my clients know other people in the same niche. This one thing alone all but eliminated my need to try to find clients, since most of my work was via word of mouth.

Having an area of specialty also makes it easier to attend industry-specific events, network with influencers online, and so on. When you keep showing up at these events or commenting on blogs and YouTube videos focused on a specific industry, people will begin to reach out to you even if no one else recommends you.

Continually Build Your Expertise

In addition to the two previously mentioned perks, the more you write content for others on a topic, the more you build your expertise in that area. I already mentioned having expert status, but expert status isn't a static thing. The longer you're in the business, and the longer you specialize in a specific field, the more your expertise grows. You can use that expertise to benefit other writing clients, and you can also use it to write your own blog and books on the same topic.

Determine Your Area of Focus

But the question is, what topic or industry should you focus on?

Brainstorm Your Skills and Interests

I recommend that you do the following exercise.

Set a timer for 15 minutes and jot down your skills, experience, and interests.

Don't be afraid to include hobbies in this, because there are a lot of hobby-related sites that may need to hire writers!

When you're doing this exercise, don't worry about whether things are related, and whether you feel they'd be profitable. Just write down any idea that comes to mind as quickly as you can.

Once the timer goes off, circle any related ideas. For example, living in Colorado, I might jot down hiking, Denver, and skiing. Those are related since you can do all of them in Colorado. Another example is that I love cooking Indian food, baking bread, and making smoothies. Those are all related to cooking.

Of those idea groups, make a list of your top three topics. I suggest three rather than just one because, at the beginning, you won't know which option will be most profitable for you.

As an example, when I was first going to go into business for myself, because I was working for a Christian non-profit at the time, I considered writing for churches and ministries. But I was also interested in blogging, digital marketing, and other aspects of writing.

As I'll share a bit later when I cover the topic of landing your first clients, I ended up landing Amy Porterfield as my first client. She and her colleagues all published content on social media, blogging, and other aspects of online marketing. Landing her as my first client gave me direction in terms of determining my area of specialty. An additional consideration was that people in business often have bigger budgets than nonprofits and churches, and since this was how I was to make a living, I had to consider which was the more profitable option.

You can also make a note of ways that you can use those topics to offer services to writing clients. For example, since I focused on online marketers, I could potentially increase my income by also offering social media management in addition to writing.

What to Do If You're Still Unsure

While I think I've made a case for why you should specialize, and how to go about finding an area of specialty, I don't want you to get too hung up on this. If you feel unsure, or if you're having a hard time finding clients in your industry of choice, start with whatever opportunities come along. You can always tweak things as you go along.

The bottom line is that you don't have to have it all figured out at the beginning, but narrowing all of your ideas down to just a few will give you a good starting point when it comes to finding an area of specialty.

Chapter 4: Choose a Business Model

In this chapter, we'll dive into how to choose a business model. I'll present several options, but by all means, if you have other ideas, don't feel compelled to stick with this list. This list is intended to provide examples and to get the wheels turning in your head regarding the type of business model that may be a good fit for you.

Without further ado, let's get into some of the business model options you might want to consider.

Work Through a Middleman

Later in this book, I provide some practical tips for landing your first clients. One of the best ways is to work for an agency. By agencies, I mean companies such as Fiverr or Upwork.

When you work through an agency, they serve as a middleman. For the most part, they help you find clients in that they add you to their marketplace. The clients pay the agency directly, and the agency, in turn, pays you. Naturally, the agency takes a cut of the payment. The reduction in pay is one of the most significant drawbacks of working for an agency, but it can be a great way to start, especially if you're having a hard time finding clients on your own.

Another huge plus of working for an agency is that you can technically get started without even having a website or social media presence. You also don't have to worry about other technical issues, such as setting up payment processing.

Go it Alone

If you decide to go it alone, you'll be responsible for finding your own clients. The disadvantage to this is that you may find it hard to find work, but the advantage is that rather than forfeiting a percentage of your pay to a middleman, all of the pay goes to you. In addition to that, at the bare minimum, you'll need a website and a way to receive payment. The good news is, there are simple (and even free) options for setting up a website, and you can also market yourself on social media, technically for free. (You may need to pay for ads to help promote your business.)

When it comes to payment processing, PayPal is the easiest way to go about getting paid. You can even send invoices to your clients through PayPal, and if you have a business account can accept payment via credit card. GoDaddy Bookkeeping and FreshBooks are also good options for keeping track of income and expenses and for sending invoices.

In terms of which option is best for you, it depends on whether you like pounding the pavement and finding clients, and feel comfortable dealing with the technological aspects yourself. (You can hire help if needed, but you may not have the budget for that when first starting.)

I've personally never worked through an agency, so the "go it alone" approach worked for me. I have friends that have used sites such as Upwork to build their entire business. The cool thing is that this isn't an all or nothing thing. You can sign up for an agency (or multiple agencies) while at the same time working to find clients on your own.

Create Content Bundles

Next, are content bundles. The idea here is to write an entire bundle of content on a specific topic such as dog grooming, gardening, and so on. The bundle can include everything from blog posts to emails to landing pages and lead magnets to eBooks. With this approach, you essentially hand clients "content in a box" for their business, and they can schedule it out in whatever ways makes the most sense to them.

Here are the pros and cons of this type of approach. The advantage is that you can sell a whole heap of content at one time to a client. The disadvantage is that you may need to write it ahead of time and then try to sell it. If you write it ahead of time, you may have to slightly tweak it to fit the client's business and desires. Clients may also balk at the high price of paying for all the content at once, and you may have to sell the bundles at much lower rates than you would get if you sold the pieces individually. Think of it as giving a bulk discount.

There are a couple of ways around these challenges. One is that you can rewrite the same basic content for multiple clients. You do need to be careful with this and make sure that you solidly rewrite everything. For instance, you can use the same research notes but start from scratch with the actual writing.

Another option is to turn this into PLR (Private Label Rights) content. PLR content is content that you sell to multiple people, with the idea that they will tweak it and add their own branding.

This article does a good job of going into the pros and cons of PLR content: https://www.skylarkvirtualservices.com/plrcontent/. Note that the pros and cons in the article pertain to the pros and cons of using PLR content compared with the pros and cons of creating and selling it. You can also check out this site for examples of PLR content others have created: https://www.plrcontentstudio.com/plrcontent-store/. Note: I haven't purchased PLR content from this company and therefore, can't vouch for it. I'm sharing it primarily so you can see how another company handles PLR content.

Create Custom Writing Packages

When you create custom writing packages, you find out what the client needs and set up a writing package specifically for them. The way that I've handled this is to have an interview with the client and find out the type of content they're looking for, as well as learn what they hope to accomplish with their content. I generally do this over the phone and take notes during the conversation.

After the conversation is complete, I write up a couple of content plan proposals, including price. Note that it helps to discuss budget during the interview or perhaps even before you have the conversation, so you have some idea what type of packages to offer. Depending on what I sense from the client in terms of their reluctance or limited ability to spend money, I create between one and three content package proposals. The value of this is that there may be less pushback compared to if you offer them just one high-priced proposal. The different packages help them to weigh their options and determine whether added services are worthwhile. It's best to reserve things like personal coaching, a lot of phone calls, etc. to the highest packages since those take more of your time and can reduce the amount of flexibility in your day.

If you opt to provide just one proposal, be prepared to remove some of the options from the proposal if they balk at the price. For example, if they say, "That's more than I expected," or "We don't have the budget for that," you can then offer to remove some of the services and come in at a lower cost.

Blogging Your Voice

As I mentioned in chapter 2, the way that my Blogging Your Voice service worked is that I interviewed clients and then wrote blog posts based on the interviews.

I asked the clients to do some prep work before the interviews so that the interview would go more smoothly and be more profitable. For example, I'd ask them to provide a working title for the post. Note that this was indeed a working title, and I often tweaked it to make it more compelling and more search engine optimized. I then asked them to jot down at least three to five main points as well as make a note of any stories they might have to share that relate to the topic.

Once we got on the phone, I talked them through the post. For example, I would say something like, "Now let's talk about five easy ways to get your baby to sleep at night. The first point is _____. Can you explain to me how to do _____?" If they used terminology that wasn't familiar to me or that may not be familiar to their readers, I asked them to explain what it means.

For instance, I would say something like, "You mentioned the term "swaddling." Can you explain what that means?" I would then ask any follow-up questions that came up either during the initial conversation or during their explanation. If they didn't tell any stories, I would ask for stories or examples of how something worked in the past for them or someone else they know. The main idea here is to get as much information from the person, in their words, so you can then write the post based on their expertise, with their voice.

By the way, I strongly recommend that you record these interviews (with the client's knowledge, of course) and either transcribe them yourself or have them transcribed. Transcription is an additional cost or time demand, but it pays off when it comes to getting the details and "voice" correct.

Obviously, you don't want to just give them a transcript of the interview. You want to tweak the wording so that it is well-written and grammatically correct. You may also rearrange the information they provided you in a way that flows better. This often happens if the person remembers things they forgot to say earlier. For example, they may say, "Oh, one other thing on the point on swaddling. . ." and when they tell you that you are already three points beyond that. You'd weave that additional information into the right point even though it came up later in the interview.

The thing that I love about the Blogging Your Voice service is that you can technically build an entire business on it. I set up packages based on one, two, or three blog posts per week, and had them pay for a month's worth of blog posts in advance. Once I received the payment, I set up the interview. Another tip is that I provided one price for one month's worth of blog posts (with no ongoing commitment) and a bit lower price for a three-month minimum commitment. I never had anyone opt for the shorter-term option.

One great thing about Blogging Your Voice is that you don't technically have to specialize in one industry. For instance, my Blogging Your Voice clients ranged from personal finance to legal to entrepreneurship, to blogging. Since I conducted interviews and had opportunities to ask questions during the interview, I didn't have to know anything about the topic before I got on the call. In fact, in some ways, it was good if I didn't know anything about the subject because that made it easier for me to notice when the client said something that an average reader might not understand.

Hire a Content Team

The first option I provided in this chapter had to do with getting work through a middleman. It's possible for you to instead BE the middleman on a small or large basis.

You can technically not do any of the writing yourself, or just do some of it. For example, with my Blogging Your Voice service, I hired other writers to write the content. Since I felt responsible for making sure the content was done right, I still handled the interviews and did the final edit of the material. The clients paid me directly, and I paid a set amount to each of the writers I hired. I've also provided book formatting services and sometimes done the work myself and other times hired people to do the formatting for the client.

There can be significant advantages to hiring other people to do the work. For one thing, you can take on a much higher volume of work than you can do on your own. Even though you must pay the people you hire, you still increase your bottom line since you only pay them a percentage of the amount that you charge the client. I can't tell you the exact percentage, as that depends mostly on how much you charge the clients and how much you need to pay other content creators to do their part of the work. If you decide to go this route, you may need to experiment a bit to get pricing and compensation amounts dialed in.

You can also hire people to do aspects of the work that you can't or don't want to do. For instance, if you have clients that are interested in starting a podcast, you can hire an audio editor to edit the audio, and you can write the show notes.

While I've hired workers to help with content production, I learned that I didn't like managing a team. Since it was my business, I felt responsible for every piece of content that was created and offered through my company, so I was never able to disconnect from the work completely. I know others that love managing a team and find hiring others to be a great way to increase income. If you decide to go this route, I recommend starting small, getting systems in place, and if things go well, branching out from there.

Retainer Vs. One-Off Projects

The next decision you need to make when it comes to your business model is whether to work on retainer or to do one-off projects. There are pros and cons to each option, but before I dive into them, let me start by explaining what I mean by "retainer." According to BusinessDictionary.com, a retainer is *"a fee paid to a person or firm to secure the privilege of obtaining its services as and when required."*

I mostly worked on a retainer basis, with some one-off projects sprinkled in to periodically boost my income. Here's how it worked for me. I agreed to work a set number of hours each month for a fixed price OR, I agreed to do a specific list of tasks each month for a set amount.

The benefit of working on a retainer basis is that my pay was essentially just as steady as it had been when I had a regular job. I knew how much money I'd make each month, based on the agreements I had with clients on retainer. For example, let's say that I had five clients, on retainer. One might pay me $500 per month, another $1,500 per month, another $350 per month, another $2,000 per month, and another $750 per month. With this example, I'd bring in a total of $5100 every month. I might also take on some one-off projects such as editing a book to bring in even more income, but I was guaranteed to make a set amount every month from my clients on retainer.

The guaranteed income every month was a significant boost to me, particularly since when I quit my day job, my husband was unemployed. Without retainer work, I would have felt less secure about freelancing full-time.

Having said that, there are some downsides to retainer work. The biggest is that in no small degree, you are tied down in similar ways as when you have a regular job. Unfortunately, in contrast to a regular job, you don't have certain benefits such as healthcare and paid time off.

One-off projects are much more flexible than working on retainer. For instance, you can take on large amounts of work (if available) during certain seasons, and less in others. If you have children in school and want to work less in the summer, you can do so by simply limiting your availability in the summer. You can also take on only the projects that interest you the most and turn down ones that aren't a good fit. The obvious downside is that your income may be very sporadic, especially in the beginning. You might finish a big project, and then have nothing or very little in the works for a while. This is very challenging, especially if you or your family depends on the income to pay bills. (This isn't such a big deal if your writing income pays for extras such as saving up for a vacation.)

The biggest thing to consider when it comes to determining if retainer or one-off projects are right for you is what matters to you most - steady income or flexibility. If regular income matters most, then working on a retainer basis is probably your best bet. If you need flexibility and can deal with a less stable income, then one-off projects are likely a good fit.

Here's the good news. This doesn't have to be an all or nothing thing. You can take on just one or two clients on retainer to give you a base salary and then take on smaller projects as they arise or in times when you have more significant financial needs and more time.

Chapter 5: Choose a Business Style

In this chapter, I get into how to choose a business style that is right for you. We've already covered types of writing you want to do, how to select an area of specialty, and how to choose a business model. While all those steps are essential, it's also important to figure out the business style that works for you.

Your business style is HOW you want to do the work. For example:

- Do you want to work behind the scenes where only the client knows you're doing the work, or do you prefer a more public role?
- Do you want to work for local, national, or international clients?
- Do you want to be part of a team, or do you prefer to work mostly in isolation?
- Do you prefer a lot of face-to-face time with clients, where you go into their office regularly, or do you prefer to be remote, and possibly never meet clients in person?
- Do you want to have one or two big clients, or do you prefer several smaller clients?

By the way, I've done both working for multiple clients and having just a few big clients. There are pros and cons to each option.

If you have a couple of big clients, and you lose one, that's a significant blow to your income, so if you choose this option, be sure to build up a substantial emergency fund. On the other hand, if you have several small clients and you lose one, it's not a huge financial blow. However, with several small clients, you can feel pulled in a million different directions.

If your writing business evolves as mine did, you may find that you experience most, if not all, the options I mentioned earlier in this book.

If you're uncertain as to which option works best for you, take whatever comes along that you find interesting. As you do the work, you'll figure out what you do and don't like and over time, be able to nail down a solid business model and style.

Chapter 6: Lay the Foundations for Healthy Client Work

The next important step on your journey to landing and working with freelance writing clients is to lay a proper foundation for building healthy client relationships.

I have a complete book on this topic, which includes how to avoid toxic clients, so in this chapter, I'll recap some of the main points. To go deeper, I recommend reading this book, which you can get here: https://www.amazon.com/Same-Page-Freelance-Relationships-Profitable-ebook/dp/B07TM9L9BR

Now let's get into a brief recap of the main points that I cover in the book.

Interview Potential Clients

First, you want to interview potential clients. You may think that as the freelancer, it's you that's being interviewed, and to some degree that is true. But it's also essential for you to determine whether the client is one for whom you want to work. Having a conversation with them to find out their expectations and work style will help you avoid a client that's not a good fit.

Get it in Writing

Once you determine you want to work for someone, be sure to put everything in writing. For instance, what you'll do, when you'll do it, and payment terms. This will help you avoid misunderstandings.

Get Paid on Time

Obviously, you want to receive payment on time for the work you do. Clients may be reluctant to pay 100% upfront, so a good compromise is to be paid 50% before you start the work, and the balance upon the completion of the project. If you do retainer work, you can set up recurring billing.

Train Your Clients

Next, let's talk about training your clients. What I mean by training your clients is that the actions you take as a freelancer teach your clients to expect and then demand certain behaviors of you. For instance, if you say that you take evenings and weekends off, and yet respond to emails quickly 24/7, despite what you've said, you're training your clients to expect immediate responses from you. Sadly, once clients get used to certain behaviors, it's tough to reverse things. Therefore, be sure that your actions with your clients line up with your values.

Position Yourself to Fire Clients

Next, it's crucial to position yourself to fire clients that are either abusive or not a good fit in other ways. The two most common ways to go about that are to have multiple clients so you can afford to fire someone. If you work for just a handful of clients, build up a substantial emergency fund so that you can afford to fire a client without stressing about how you're going to pay your bills.

Chapter 7: Find Your First Clients

In this chapter, we'll get into how to find your first clients.

Do Limited Amounts of Work for Free

I'm generally not a big fan of doing work for free, but it can be worthwhile to do some work for free, in limited quantities.

That's how I got started working for Amy Porterfield. I noticed some typos in some of her sales copy and reached out to her to offer 50 pages of free editing. She took me up on the offer, and as she got to know me, decided to hire me.

If you offer to do this, know that there's no guaranteed that you'll be hired, but you can ask for a testimonial for your website and LinkedIn profile. To keep from getting burned, be clear about the limited nature of the work you'll do for free.

Put the Word Out

Let everyone you know that you are looking for clients and the type of work you are most interested in doing.

And by the way, when I say everyone, I mean everyone. Don't underestimate the importance of letting friends and family members know what you're doing. Just because they don't run a business doesn't mean that they don't know business owners.

When you meet people, and they ask what you do, let them know you write. Don't use words that make you sound less than professional. For instance, rather than say, "I'm an aspiring writer," with confidence, say, "I'm a writer." If you do some writing – even if only on your own blog – you don't need permission to call yourself a writer.

Build a Portfolio of Your Work

Next, build a portfolio of your work. This is one of the many benefits of having a blog. While you're still waiting for clients (and for that matter, beyond that time), publish your best work on your blog. To help establish credibility, be sure to post content consistently. Treat your blog as if it was a paid gig.

If you've chosen an area of expertise, as mentioned in chapter 3, consider writing a book on the topic to help establish your expert status.

You can also write guests posts. This is yet another reason to choose an industry focus. The more you blog on a topic, the more you're seen as an expert, which increases the opportunities you'll have as a guest blogger.

Most guest blogging opportunities offer a chance to include an author bio with links to your website. In the bio, include the fact that you're a freelance writer specializing in "x" topic.

Establish a Social Media Presence

It's not technically necessary to have a raving fanbase on social media. I've landed client work mainly through my blog, not social media.

Let me shoot straight with you about my experience with social media. I struggle with it. A lot. It just doesn't float my boat. One of my biggest struggles with it is that I find it hard to do consistently. Because of that, I've decided to focus more on writing instead of putting much time into social media.

Having said that, social media has a place. For instance, you may indeed use it to establish a fanbase, or you may use it to interact with other writers or people in your target market. This type of interaction often happens in Facebook groups since they tend to have a particular area of focus.

That's how I use Facebook. I'm in Facebook groups on a near-daily basis. I use the platform to build relationships and network with other writers. This is a huge help when it comes to support and encouragement. Through my relationships with other writers on Facebook, I often have people who give me honest feedback, encourage me when I hit hard times, read and review my books and so on.

One last bit of advice when it comes to social media. Figure out what platform resonates the most with you and put most of your social media time and energy into that one platform. For example, I mentioned earlier that I struggle with being consistent on social media. With most social media sites, that's a big problem. But guess what? Pinterest is considered a bookmarking site rather than a social media site. Bookmarking I can do. And while Google is my number one source of blog traffic overall, Pinterest is now my number one source of referral traffic.

I share my struggles with social media so that you'll know that you can create a social media plan that works for you. I get encouragement and support from my writer-friends on Facebook, and I drive traffic to my site by spending limited amounts of time on Pinterest. I spend the rest of my business-building time merely writing. Your social media presence will likely look very different from mine. The critical thing is to figure out what works best for you and don't let people guilt you into trying to be active on every social media platform.

Sign Up for Freelancing Sites

In chapter 4, when I covered choosing a business model, one of the options that I shared is to find writing clients through an intermediary. Here are some of the best options for finding writing gigs through freelancing sites.

Upwork (https://upwork.com) is the best-known site for freelancers, including writers. Now to be fair, people pitch their writing services from all over the world, sometimes at ridiculously low rates. The good news is, while you may have to start at low rates, as your reputation grows, so can your pricing.

Fiverr (https://fiverr.com) is, as the name implies, based on gigs that pay $5. Whoopee? Obviously, there's a healthy limit to what you can do for only $5. Having said that, Fiverr now also allows some higher-paying gigs, so it's worth checking out. Also, as is often the case, you can use a platform like Fiverr as a way of getting your name out there and potentially landing higher-paying work outside of Fiverr. I do know some freelancers that swear by Fiverr, so don't dismiss it outright without looking into it a bit further. If you like what you see, experiment with it.

Here are some other job boards to consider.

First, ProBlogger.com/Jobs https://problogger.com/jobs/

At the current time, there are freelance writing jobs available on the ProBlogger job board from all over the world, and many of them are location independent.

AllFreelanceWriting.com
https://allfreelancewriting.com/freelance-writing-jobs/

Currently has jobs ranging from the low pay range of $25-$50, to the semi-pro range of $50-$100, to the pro rate of $100 - $250.

BloggingPro.com - https://www.bloggingpro.com/jobs/

Currently has everything from scriptwriting to fashion blogging, to someone needed to write ukulele-related content.

Contena.co https://www.contena.co/

Currently has work ranging from video tutorial game writing to fitness writing, to science writing and more.

You can also follow writing job profiles on Twitter. Here are three good ones to consider.

@write_jobs https://twitter.com/write_jobs - @write_jobs

@WhoPaysWriters https://twitter.com/WhoPaysWriters

@jjobs_tweets https://twitter.com/jjobs_tweets

Reach Out to Potential Clients

Next, let's talk about reaching out to potential clients. This option may seem scary, and it can be, particularly if they've never even heard of you.

But I've found more than one job by deciding what type of job I wanted, and then cold calling the company to see if they are hiring.

It's incredible how often they "just happened" to have had a conversation about needing someone just like me right before I contacted them.

Before making a call, or reaching out via email, do a bit of research into the company so that you can be specific in your pitch. For instance, rather than saying something generic such as, "Your site needs a blog, and I can help," give them some specific feedback and ideas for the type of content you can create for them. When you do this, refer to the actual content on their site, or information you know about their business if you've visited in person. When you reach out, use a professional email address with a link to your blog or LinkedIn profile so that they can see samples of your work.

As a side note, let me say that I get email pitches regularly from people that want me to hire them to work on my site. The emails are generally very generic, and it's clear they know nothing about my business. These emails also often come from Gmail accounts, and they typically don't include a link to their site, so there is no domain name for me to check out. Do you know what I do with those emails? I delete them.

As rude as it may seem, I don't even give the people the courtesy of a response. The reason for this is simple. If a person reaches out to me to pitch their business and they don't even bother to take the time to learn about me and tailor their email to me and my business, I consider the email spam and unworthy of my time. Therefore, keep that in mind when you send unsolicited pitches for your writing services.

Network with Other Writers

I touched on this briefly earlier when I brought up joining Facebook groups. Become an active participant in Facebook groups that focus on freelance writing. Look for ways to help others in the group, and as opportunities arise, share about the types of writing clients you desire.

Build Relationships with People in Your Industry Focus

Comment on blogs and YouTube videos, and attend conferences and networking events specific to your chosen industry. For example, if you want to specialize in writing content for faith-based organizations, in addition to church attendance, go to Christian conferences. If you're going to write pet-related articles, chat it up with people in your local pet store, and attend every pet-related event in your area.

It takes time to build relationships, but over time you'll become known as THE writer for the industry, and you'll likely be the one that comes to mind when someone is looking for a writer. By the way, this approach is another excellent reason to specialize.

I trust that this chapter gave you some good ideas for where to find your first freelance writing clients. If you're feeling overwhelmed, the good news is that you don't need to do all of these to succeed. I recommend picking two or three that resonate the most with you and going all-in with them.

Once you start landing clients, don't forget to ask them for testimonials and referrals, which is something I'll get into in the next chapter on laying the foundation for growing your writing business.

Chapter 8: Set the Stage for Growing Your Writing Business

Once you land your first clients, it's important to lay the foundation for continually growing your freelance writing business. Even the best clients don't typically last forever. Either you get tired of doing the work, or as their business changes and your business changes, they are no longer a good fit for you. I've also experienced times when clients have hit a bump in the road in their own business and can no longer afford my services. The bottom line is that it's essential to put things in place that make it easier to land new clients.

Gather Testimonials

If you only do one thing to grow your business, I recommend gathering testimonials from every client, even if the job you did for them was small. Recommendations from others, be it a personal recommendation from a client, or testimonials on a website, can go a long way toward gaining the trust of potential clients and customers.

Here's just one personal example of how this worked for me.

After finishing a project for a brand new client, I asked, "How did you hear about me?" She responded, "I noticed you from a guest post you did on Amy Porterfield's site. I liked that you were thorough and professional. When I went to your site, the Pat Flynn testimonial put me over the top. I'm a big fan of his, and I know that he has his stuff together and wouldn't just recommend anyone."

Notice how the thing that first got her attention was that my blog post was "thorough and professional," which underscores the importance of good quality content. But the thing that put her over the top was the testimonial. This is an excellent example of how content such as blog posts, combined with testimonials, can build trust and lead to sales.

As a side note, before I continue, I want to say that I've been fortunate to have some big-name clients recognized in the world of online business. That has no doubt helped as people are sometimes impressed if they recognize the name of someone on my testimonials page. But never, ever feel that testimonials from "everyday" people don't count.

Now let's get into how to get testimonials from your clients. The good news is, it's not as hard as you might think. Here are a few things that I've found help tremendously.

Provide Services That Are "Testimonial Worthy"

Let's face it if your services or products stink, people aren't going to want to provide testimonials for you. So, the first step in gaining testimonials is to always, at the bare minimum, do what you promise, or even better, go the extra mile and exceed the expectations of your clients. If you find that you're embarrassed to ask for a testimonial, it could be that you're not confident in the quality of what your business provides, and if that's the case, that's the first thing you need to fix. This brings me to my next point:

Ask for the Testimonial

While some people may voluntarily provide a testimonial without prompting, most will not — even if they are delighted with your products or services. However, I have found that in most cases, even very busy people will provide a testimonial when asked — if they are happy with the work you did for them or the products they purchased from you.

Tip: Ask for a testimonial right away, as soon as you complete a project. People feel the most positive about you right after you finished work for them, particularly if you've hit the ball out of the park on the project. I've found it helpful to send a thank you email to let a client know that I appreciated the opportunity to do the work for them, and then let them know that it would mean a lot to me if they would provide a testimonial.

Make it Easy for the Person to Write the Testimonial

Next, it's important to make it easy for the person to write the testimonial. I believe there are two main reasons why people may not provide a testimonial for you, even if they are happy with you. First, a lot of people get stuck and don't know what to say. This is especially true if they haven't written testimonials before, or if they don't like to write. Second, people are busy and may have good intentions, but never quite get around to writing the testimonial for you.

I've found a solution that has, up to this point, worked 100% of the time for me; I provide a short series of questions for the person to answer, with the offer to write the testimonial for them, once they give the answers. This has worked great for me because people often respond immediately after receiving the email from me because it is so easy and takes them only a few minutes. The questions I ask are:

- List 3 things you liked about the product or service
- Would you recommend this product or service to others? Why?
- Is there anything else you'd like to add?

I also ask for a photo, and what website they'd like me to use.

I then write the testimonial based on their responses to the questions. This is a natural process for those of us that write! I then send the testimonial to them for their approval before posting it on my site.

How to Verify That the Testimonials on Your Site Are Legit

Let's deal with the elephant in the room. There can be skepticism regarding testimonials on a website. After all, a business owner could write anything and put it on a website. But there are a few ways to give people peace of mind regarding the validity of the testimonials. **Here are a few ideas to get you started:**

- Include both a first and last name. You may not be able to do this if the service or product you provide would embarrass people in some way, but for most businesses, this shouldn't be a problem.
- Include a photo of the person. If you're unable to obtain a picture of the person, their logo will do, but unless the company is well known, it's not as ideal, since photos feel more personal.
- Include a link to their website.

Also, since it is now easy for people to check your business out online, whenever possible, have the same testimonials posted places that you don't control, such as LinkedIn. I didn't do this at the beginning, but after writing the testimonial, I now send a request for a recommendation via LinkedIn. Since the testimonial has already been written, it takes just a few minutes for the person to help me out in this way, and assuming they are on LinkedIn, most are happy to do so.

Chapter 9: Top 5 Mistakes Freelance Writers Make

Mistakes. We all make them. That's the bad news. The good news is that we can learn from the mistakes that others make and hopefully avoid making them ourselves. In this chapter, I dive into the five most common mistakes that new freelance writers make.

Self-Doubt

Self-doubt is a common mistake of many, if not all, new freelance writers. It plagues many writers, including seasoned ones. I know that I struggle with self-doubt myself.

Imposter Syndrome

I suffer from something known as "imposter syndrome." Imposter syndrome is something that hits highly competent people who, despite their accomplishments, feel like their success is based on luck or other factors, rather than skill, hard work, and so on. The "imposter" idea is related to feeling like you're not as good as people think you are and that any day now, you'll be exposed as a fraud.

While I still struggle with this, my husband helped me overcome this by asking me a simple question. He said, "Do you think all the people you've worked for are wrong?" He went on to name well-known, highly successful people I've had as clients who all love me and rave about my work. His question, in a sense, brought their expertise and wisdom into question, and I had to admit that it was highly unlikely that I had been able to pull the wool over the eyes of all these amazingly talented and successful people.

You may not have a supportive spouse like I do, but if you struggle with imposter syndrome, I want you to spend a few minutes thinking about all of the words of affirmation spoken to you by friends, family members, employers, coworkers, and any clients you've had. If you find it helpful, do this exercise in your journal. List every positive thing that people tend to say about you such as, "hardworking, attention to detail, fast worker, pleasant to work with," and so on. Then ask yourself if all those people are wrong about what they say about you. Chances are, they are not!

In addition to this, I recommend keeping a file of positive feedback you receive from others. This can be a paper or an electronic file. Then, every time you get a pat on the back from someone put it in that file. If you use a paper file, when you receive words of affirmation online such as in email, print it off and put it in the file. If you keep an electronic file and receive a physical piece of affirmation such as a thank-you card, take a picture of it and add it to your electronic file. Periodically review those words of affirmation to keep those negative thoughts at bay. If you're creative, you can even make a physical or digital scrapbook of the positive things people have said about you. The point is, get into the habit of paying attention to and believing the fantastic things people say about you.

"I'm Not Good Enough"

In some ways, the feelings of not being good enough can relate to imposter syndrome. However, they can also be rooted in the truth. Before you feel discouraged, let me assure you that I'm referring to fixable things, not your overall worth as a person or writer. For instance, there are no doubt writers out there that are more talented than you. That is true for all of us! Maybe you tend to use a lot of passive voice in your writing, or are a terrible speller, or struggle with grammatical errors. Perhaps you don't know a lot about content marketing and don't even have a blog or website yet. Maybe you have no social media following.

All these things can have a measure of truth to them when it comes to feelings of inadequacy. The critical thing to keep in mind is that even if you lack skills in certain areas, that doesn't mean that you aren't good enough. It merely means that you have room for improvement. Join the club!

Now I don't want to diminish the need for improvement. We shouldn't brush aside our shortcomings by giving ourselves a pep talk. However, we can use words such as "yet" when describing shortcomings. For instance, you can admit to yourself that, "I'm not good at writing in active voice, yet." Or, "My grammar skills aren't yet what they need to be." You can even add to that a simple statement of intent for improving them. For example, "My grammar skills aren't yet what they need to be, but I'm taking a Skillshare class to help me improve in this area. By the end of the year, my grammar skills will be up to par." (As a side note, I mentioned Skillshare because it's my favorite online learning platform. It's very affordable, and there are thousands of classes available. To get a free two-month trial, use my referral link: https://professionalcontentcreation.com/skillshare.)

One thing that I've found helpful is to give an honest assessment of my lack of skills in a particular area and then make a commitment to gradual improvement in that one area. This is similar to the Japanese concept of Kaizen. The word "Kaizen" means to make a change for the better. The actual definition of the word doesn't include the idea of gradual improvement. However, the Toyota corporation used the word in such a way as to encourage employees to make continual, gradual improvement.

Let's look at the two key words: continual and gradual. Continual means this is something you do on an ongoing basis. Gradual means that you're not trying to make vast improvements all at once. Instead, set a goal to make tiny improvements regularly.

For example, let's say that you struggle with grammar. You don't know how to use punctuation marks, and you have no idea why you put commas where you do. Pick just one item and learn how to do it properly, and then practice proper use. Using commas as an example, read up on proper comma usage in English handbooks so that you get a grasp on how to use them. Then, in everything you write for an entire month, check your comma usage. Sentence by sentence, check to see if you've used commas properly. Keep referring to the English handbook to check your comma usage.

During this month of comma focus, don't get hung up on worrying about writing in active voice or how to properly use quotation marks. Those things can come later. Just focus on becoming excellent at one thing - commas. When using commas properly becomes second nature, add in the next thing. Make this type of gradual improvement a regular part of your growth as a writer. Before you know it, you'll be a truly skilled writer. And by the way, while you're in the process, instead of internally saying, "I'm not good enough," say something like, "My grammar skills need improvement, but my skills are improving every single day. I'll be a grammar pro in no time!"

Feeling Like It's Too Late

Another common area of self-doubt is feeling that it's too late. You may feel that it's too late to start a blog. Your internal dialog may be something like, "Maybe if I started a blog ten years ago, I'd have a shot, but it's too late. There's no hope for me." The reality is that few of us start at the optimal time.

I'm famous for being slow to jump into new things. For example, I wanted to be a writer when I graduated from high school but didn't submit my first magazine articles until almost 20 years later. My husband tried to get me to write books, but I didn't feel that I had enough to say to write books, so ignored his encouragement for years. Unless you're an early adopter, chances are that you're "behind," on every social media platform out there.

Here's the truth. Early adopters have an easier time than those that start later. But that doesn't mean that it's too late. I'll give you a personal example. I already mentioned that I don't love social media. So, I pretty much ignored it, even though I knew I "should" do it. Just a couple of months ago, I decided to give Pinterest a try - nine long years after it started. Am I too late? Is it possible for me to use Pinterest effectively? No and yes. No, I'm not too late, and yes, I can use Pinterest effectively - even though I'm "late."

One huge thing to keep in mind is not to compare yourself with others, and instead only compete with yourself. To add a bit of clarity to the Pinterest discussion, I started Pinterest quite a few years ago. I set up a profile, pinned a few things, etc. I probably spent a couple of weeks on it and quit. When I decided to give it an honest try a couple of months ago, I had

27 monthly viewers. Yes, 27. Pathetic! As I write this, I have 42,000 monthly viewers. Now, to be honest, that is "terrible" compared to people who are successful on Pinterest. In fact, I've noticed people that have two million monthly viewers. If I worry about "catching up" to those people, I may indeed be too late. The deal is, I don't have to catch up to those people. I just need to use Pinterest to help drive traffic to my blog, and if I'm improving in that, I'm not too late.

What I want you to come away with is that while you may struggle more and your growth may be slower if you are starting a freelance writing business in a field that is saturated, that doesn't mean it's too late. It may mean that you need to work harder and longer to find the success you desire. Or you may need to niche down to tap into a field that isn't overly saturated. But it's never too late for those who are willing to put in the necessary work to build a freelance writing business.

Believing that Failure is Fatal

As if dealing with the issue of self-doubt isn't enough, despite your best efforts, at times, you will fail. That's not a reflection on you. It's something we all experience.

You may spend a lot of time reaching out to a potential client, have a solid phone call or two with them, and in spite of all your hard work and how positive they seemed to feel about you, in the end, they decided to hire someone else.

Even worse, let's say you land the gig, and you can't make them happy. Maybe they even tell you that your writing stinks or that you're not worth the money. That could be a bad, unreasonable client, but such rejection still stings. Going even deeper, let's say that you are hired to work a big project, and you totally bomb. And I don't mean that the client was unreasonable, I mean that you just couldn't do it. You bit off more than you can chew, or it was beyond your skill level. No matter how hard you worked, you couldn't complete the assignment. The bottom line is that you failed. Wow, that hurts. It stings almost more than anything in the professional world. But it's not fatal. Regardless of your failures, there is hope for the future.

Here are a few ways that I've found to overcome failures.

Not All Clients Are a Good Fit

First of all, recognize that not all clients are a good fit. It doesn't necessarily mean that there is something wrong with you or with them. Think of it like a dating relationship or friendship. Not everyone you connect with is the right choice for a lifelong partner or best friend. Sometimes things click, and sometimes they don't. That's not failure; it's just life. So, if you pitch to a client and they reject you, embrace the fact that the client or position wasn't right for you, and move on.

Own Up to Mistakes

There are times when you can't blame your failure on someone else. These are times that go beyond a client not being a good fit or being unreasonable. They are times when you truly mess up. Be honest about those failures, both with yourself and with the client.

Learn from Mistakes and Move On

Once you've owned up to the fact that you've made a mistake, take some time to ponder what went wrong. For example, did you take on a project that in your gut you knew wasn't a good fit? Did you act like you knew how to do something when you didn't? Did you overcommit and put yourself in a position where there was no way you could get the work done on time?

Let me be clear that the point of this self-analysis isn't to beat yourself up or wallow in your failure. The point is to learn from your mistakes, so you don't make the same mistakes again. Once you learn from them, put them aside and move on. Don't let those failures define you. The failure is a thing that happened, but it's not the final word on who you are and the value you have to offer to the world. Learn from your mistakes, brush yourself off, and move on.

Accepting Low-Paying Work

Another huge mistake new freelance writers make is accepting low-paying work. This may sound strange when you consider that in chapter seven, one of the tips I shared for landing your first clients is to do limited amounts of work for free. "Limited" is a keyword to keep in mind. In the beginning, you may need to do some work for free or for a low price, to get some experience and testimonials. Just don't settle for low-paying work over the long haul. Don't believe the lie that you aren't good enough to be paid a living wage writing.

Don't Be Afraid to Negotiate

One way to overcome the low-pay problem is to learn how to negotiate. There are a couple of ways to negotiate. The obvious one is money. Don't be afraid to ask for more money, especially if the work will be challenging or unpleasant in any way. When you think about it, negotiations happen in many aspects of life. When you walk on a car lot or into an open house, there is a posted price. That doesn't mean that you must buy the item at that price. You can offer something different than the stated price.

The way this can work as a writer is that a client may want to pay you an amount that is lower than you need to pay your bills, or even deeper than that, smaller than you feel you deserve. Don't be afraid to counter with an offer of your own. Give whatever legitimate reasons you can, without going into your problems. For instance, a new client may not care that you're a single mom and need to make "x" dollars per month to keep a roof over your head. But they will likely understand that based on your experience and the amount of time the work will take, you feel that "x" is a reasonable amount for the job. You can also lookup the going rate for similar work and share that with them, as they may not realize what the average writer will charge for that type of work.

You can also agree to do the work for a lower price for a limited amount of time. As an example, I wrote a proposal for a client that wanted to hire me on a retainer basis. In my proposal, I set a price of $4,000 per month. He responded that he was willing to pay me that, but that I needed to prove myself first. He proposed that I start at $3,000 a month and work at that rate for 90 days. At the end of 90 days, if he was pleased with my work, he'd increase my pay to $4,000 per month. I felt that was a reasonable compromise, and truth be told, when I pitched $4,000 per month, I was prepared to do the work for a minimum of $3,000 per month.

Another thing to keep in mind is that there are non-monetary ways to be compensated. For example, let's say they want to pay you less than you desire, but want you to travel and you really don't want to travel. You can negotiate the travel portion and state you are willing to work for an "x" amount without travel (or with a specific amount of limited travel) but will require an "x" amount if they expect you to travel more than a certain amount. This allows them to reevaluate what they most need. Do they want or need to pay you less, but are willing to reduce or eliminate travel? Or do they value the travel component enough to pay you more than they originally planned?

I've also heard of people negotiating based on perks the company can offer, such as the use of a company car or a company owned cabin that your family can use for vacations for free.

There are other types of valuable non-monetary compensation that are specific to writers. As an example, you can expect higher pay if they don't publicly acknowledge your work with a byline or by putting you on the company website. If you ghostwrite a book, you can ask that your name be on the cover of the book. This is free advertising and can lead to other work, so it has some value in addition to the actual payment for the work.

How to Increase Your Pay Gradually

Another thing to consider is that you can increase your pay gradually. This is one reason why you might want to limit the date range of a contract. I mention this because I've had the problem of agreeing to a certain amount of payment without any time limit on it, and technically I can end up working for the same pay rate for years. Now it is true that you can let clients know at any time that you are raising your rates, but it helps if there is a hard date when the current agreement ends.

One thing to keep in mind is that not all clients are willing to pay you more than initially agreed, so I don't suggest increasing your rates with former clients unless you're willing to have them walk away. You can also use a hybrid approach. Maintain original rates for current clients and charge more for new clients. With this approach, your overall average rate increases even if you don't raise your rates for long-term clients.

Worrying About the Competition

It's a mistake to worry too much about your competition. This often indicates a scarcity mindset. You know, the feeling that there isn't enough work to go around and that if someone else succeeds, by default, you fail. It can be true that if a client is "shopping around" for a writer, they may check you out and check out one of your competitors and end up going with the competitor. However, the flip side of this is that they may choose you over someone else.

Recognize Your Unique Value

The vital thing to keep in mind is that you have a unique value. Your personality is unique and will resonate with some people and not so much with others. Don't worry about the ones that prefer someone over you. You don't really want to work for someone that isn't a good fit, do you?

Also, your experiences and the services you offer will appeal to some and not others. This is not a bad thing! If you focus on being yourself and offering services that fit with your gifts and passions, you'll attract the right people and repel the wrong people.

Don't Compare Yourself with Others

For the most part, I strongly advise you not to compare yourself to others. You may see other writers that have popular blogs or podcasts or substantial social media followings or some other outward measure of success and feel inadequate. Maybe they talk about their six-figure earnings, and you are still trying to scrape together the money to pay your light bill or worse, to land your first client. Trust me, unless they were born with a silver spoon in their mouths (and most weren't), at one time they, too, had to land that first client and had a near-empty business bank account. They, also, may have taken on work that didn't thrill them, or struggled with any of the other things related to your current struggles.

Now I *am* a fan of comparing yourself with. . . yourself. Strive to improve upon where you are today. If you've never sent a query letter before and send your first query letter, pat yourself on the back. If you've never made any money writing and a mere $50 lands in your PayPal account from your first client, celebrate! Make it a habit to compete against yourself. Set a goal of steadily increasing different aspects of your business. For example, if you made $100 writing this month, see if you can double that next month. If you have 100 blog visitors this month, shoot for 300 next month. By the way, the numbers I'm using are arbitrary and meant as examples, not specific guidelines. The point is to make a note of where you are now, and track your progress, with the goal of *gradually* improving each area of your writing business.

Now that I've (hopefully) made that clear, I want to mention that there are times when comparing yourself with others makes sense. For instance, it helps to know the going rate for the type of writing you do. You can look on a site such as Upwork and see the hourly rate for other writers. Bear in mind, however, that everyone has different gifts, advantages, and disadvantages, and even more importantly, are at different places in the writing journey.

Not Building Your Own Platform

One of the biggest mistakes that freelance writers make is putting all their time and energy into building other people's platforms and neglecting to develop their own. I know this is true because it happened to me. In fact, I've spent so much time writing content for others, I've had no time, energy, or desire to write my content. This makes sense from the perspective that it's crucial to meet deadlines and do an excellent job for your clients.

However, there's a problem with this, and that is that when you lose clients, it may be hard to quickly find more if you've neglected to build your platform. If you haven't updated your blog or social media for months, you likely get very little exposure on those platforms. If you have an email list, but you never send emails to your list, when you do, many will forget that they signed up for your list and mark it as spam.

Also, as a writer, I like to make money writing content in my name. I do this in various ways, such as through this book you're currently reading. I also do this by writing blog content. My blog posts help sell my books and other products and bring in affiliate income. There's something very freeing about having writing income that isn't based exclusively on client work. One of the things that I like most about it is that it's often passive and brings in income regularly, even when I'm not working.

What I'd like to encourage you to do is to treat yourself as if you are one of your clients. Set up personal writing tasks with deadlines and do them even when you feel pressed for time or don't feel like writing. After all, you'd do that for your clients, so why not treat your own business with the same level of respect?

If you do only one thing, I recommend starting a blog and blogging consistently. Don't worry, you don't necessarily need to crank out massive amounts of blog posts every month. I recommend shooting for one post per week.

Secondly, I recommend setting up an email list and incorporating it into your website. I've had great results using

MailerLite, and the best part of that is that you can get started for free. Check it out here: https://professionalcontentcreation.com/mailerlite. (Note that this is an affiliate link, which means that if you choose to sign up for a paid plan, I'll get a small commission at no additional cost to you.)

Conclusion

I hope that you've found this book helpful in your journey to becoming a successful freelance writer. You have gifts. You are unique. You have something special to offer to the world and are a perfect fit for the right clients.

Stick with the plan presented in this book (and outlined below) and you'll find success.

I wish you the best in all your writing endeavors!

Writing Client Roadmap

Step 1: Consider the pros and cons of client work.

Step 2: Determine the type of writing you want to do.

Step 3: Determine an area of specialty.

Step 4: Choose a business model.

Step 5: Choose a business style.

Step 6: Lay the foundation for healthy client relationships.

Step 7: Find your first clients. (Throw a big party when this happens!)

Resources

Below is a list of resources that I've used to build my writing business. Some are free, and some cost some money, but all are reasonably priced. If it's on this list, this means that I either have in the past or currently do use the service or product and personally vouch for it. Please note that some of the links are affiliate links which means that if you purchase the item using my link, I'll receive a small commission at no additional cost to you.

Siteground

https://professionalcontentcreation.com/siteground

I recommend setting up a self-hosted WordPress website. Siteground is a good, reasonably priced webhost that I personally use. My experience with them has been excellent. Their support is timely and professional.

Thrive Themes

https://professionalcontentcreation.com/thrive

Thrive Themes is much more than just a theme for your website. It also includes everything from landing pages to optin forms to even a plugin for creating online courses. It's quickly becoming one of my favorite business-building tools.

MailerLite

https://professionalcontentcreation.com/mailerlite

If you haven't yet started an email list, or if you've started one and aren't happy with your current email service provider, I highly recommend MailerLite. Even the free account (that allows up to 1,000 subscribers) has many advanced features that are easy to use. I've also received excellent support in a timely manner from this company.

Grammarly

https://professionalcontentcreation.com/grammarly

We all make mistakes, and self-editing is a must. Grammarly is my favorite tool for catching pesky mistakes. Grammarly has both a paid and free account. I personally recommend using the paid account, but by all means, if your budget is limited, start with the free account to check it out.

Natural Reader

https://naturalreaders.com/

Listening to my written content is another way I catch mistakes. In fact, listening is the easiest way to catch little mistakes such as "it" when you meant to write "is." Listening also helps you noticed repetitive and awkwardly worded sentences.

Thank You

Thank you so much for reading my work. Please consider reviewing this book on Amazon. Reviews help others to find my books and are much appreciated.

www.ingramcontent.com/pod-product-compliance
Lightning Source LLC
Chambersburg PA
CBHW020605220526
45463CB00006B/2461